# Holding My Own

## Tim Hampton

# *Holding My Own*

-------------------------------------------------

Published by Instant Publisher ISBN 159196-552-7
2004 Tim Hampton

3

# INTRODUCTION

*When the words "prison" and "young black male" are uttered in the same sentence, society automatically assumes that a story is about to be told by another young black convicted felon, locked up behind bars, crying out for attention and pity. In the case of "Holding My Own", I am a young black man telling a story about being black and being in prison, only my viewpoint is from an officer's side. This story is based on one of the largest prison systems in the entire world. There are some serious problems with the prison system, not only in Texas, but all across the country. Before you read this book, take a minute and ask yourself, "what really goes on in there?" Have you ever found it strange that we only hear about people when they are either going to or just getting out of prison? Have you ever wondered why some people go to prison and return to society ten times worse than when they went in? How are individuals treated during their stay in prison? Finally, the guards -- how are they trained, where do they come from, and what role do they play in the criminal justice system? Holding My Own answers some of those questions from my personal experience, however, keep in mind that there are still many questions remaining that even I, Tim Hampton, cannot answer…*

On a sunny September morning, all was normal. I was walking the catwalk and conducting a security check as I usually do, making sure all inmates were alive and breathing, or simply not fighting each other or making out, as your mind might suggest when you're thinking about life in the penitentiary. My partner, Mr. Petry, a spiritual man, was working inside the control picket. His job was to open cell doors that I needed opened and to make sure I did not get clicked on by the inmates. The free-world term might be jumped or simply beat-up. Whatever you might call it, it's not what someone would want to happen to them. As I entered section B, which was the middle part of the wing and housed approximately forty-two of the one hundred and nineteen inmates I was responsible for, I heard someone yell "Look out boss -- I need to get the hell out of here!" As I approached thirty-four cell, what I saw inside was considered by many to be America's nightmare: A young black male, age Seventeen to twenty-three, six feet five inches tall, weighing about two hundred and forty pounds with five percent body fat, and absolutely no regard for authority, nor life itself. I asked him what his problem was and, again, he just yelled at me "Let me the fuck out of here!" Well, by this time, the other forty-one inmates' attention was focused on thirty-four cell and eagerly anticipating my next move. What I had learned in my earlier days of being a correctional officer is that when in a stressful, or spontaneous, situation, I was watched by many to see how I would respond. The reputation that I developed up to this point, was a hard-core ass-kicking correctional officer, who went throughout the prison unit and whipped on inmates for little or no reason at all. I had refused to take disrespect from any inmate -- and suddenly here I am, listening to this inmate yell at me making demands! If I walked away, I would be considered a punk, if I stood there and argued with this inmate, I would be considered stupid. Thinking that I was making a wise decision, I had Mr. Petry open the cell door, remove the inmate from the cell block, in order to talk to him one-on-one to try to calm him down and figure out his problem. I had absolutely no idea what I was in for. "Look at this shit, boss man -- I need to take my medicine!" I looked at an empty prescription bottle of the drug Haldol. Most of the inmates are on some type of medication. Some inmates had to go to the unit's medical department to retrieve their medication daily, however, others were allowed to get the entire prescription and keep it on them to take as needed. Whenever an inmate's medicine supply was low, it was his responsibility to request more. In this case, this inmate failed to do so and I quickly realized that this was not only an aggravated inmate, but an aggravated inmate who had not taken his anti-psychotic medicine for god knows how long!  At that time, I didn't know whether to run or fight. But during my decision process, all I could see is a right closed fist charging towards my head.  I was able to dodge the blow, and soon my natural instincts took over and I countered with one of my own. At that instance, I realized I was involved in yet another fist fight!   I remembered all the fights I was involved in during my high school days, but none were like this one with a real psycho.  I kept swinging and swinging, and I was gaining the upper hand. Knowing that my fellow officers were on the way gave me even more confidence that this situation would be over soon, and when my fellow officers arrived, they assisted me in getting the inmate to the floor and restraining him. Soon thereafter, an officer carrying a video camera came and started filming. A few seconds later, a supervisor came. I was somewhat proud of myself because when I looked at the inmate, he was bleeding from his nose and mouth, and one of his eye's were swollen. I knew that this is exactly what my supervisor wanted and expected. However, the real question lurked inside my head -- How did I get myself into this, and when will this whole thing be over?

# I

# HOW I GOT STARTED

All my life I often thought of what it would be like once I am an adult. I mean what will I become -- a preacher, a teacher, a basketball player? Never in my wildest dreams did I intend on becoming a prison guard, a young African American prison guard nevertheless. The local hospital where I was employed as a surgical assistant taught me to have pride, dignity, integrity, and the self-respect that I needed to become a well-molded citizen. My job duties included rolling a gurney to patients' rooms whom were scheduled to have some sort of surgical procedure that day. Once I returned to the surgery department with that person, I was responsible for hooking up E. K. G. machines and checking vital signs to ensure the patent's stability before he or she were given anesthetics. During certain procedures, from minor outpatient procedures to open-heart surgery, I was often called upon to deliver instruments to nurses and/or doctors as they requested them. After the procedure was completed, and once the person was out of recovery, I was responsible for returning the patient safely to his or her room. This was an extremely big advantage, considering the odds of a nineteen year old sneaker, two pierced ears, flea marketed style gold jewelry wearing black guy being dependent on and working side by side with people who spent no less than a decade in school learning how to save lives. Perfect as it may seem, reality struck hard and quick. Seems like the older I got, the more it cost to live. Sneakers and jewelry that I once used to buy at will, became more distant due to the fact that my aunt and uncle, whom I was residing with, felt it was time for me to become independent and start facing life, Just like other adults do. My aunt was a kind-hearted, extremely sensitive person who many people looked up to. She was the type of person who would give her last to a stranger. My uncle was also a kind-hearted gentleman who, when he spoke, was straight forward, and did not beat around the bush. He also worked a lot, so I did not get a chance to see him often, but he still made time to let me know that I had to move out. For days I tried to figure out why I had to move out, then a secret they knew, but I didn't, was revealed. In approximately eight months, I would be signing a birth certificate! Paranoid at first, but then the man finally came out of me. Milk, diapers, baby sitters, health insurance, all

these things were running through my mind --
"Me a Daddy?" I am not ready for this... I knew
that there was no turning back at this point. I
could not run from this situation. I am going to
be depended on by a child, my own child! I
knew it was time to make a change. You see, the
high caliber profile job that I held was paying me
a less the desirable wage of eight bucks and
forty-five cents an hour. But who's
complaining? It was my decision to not pursue
any more schooling after I graduated the twelfth
grade.

 On the rainy afternoon of Monday October 17,
1994, I went to see Ms. Savoic at the Texas
Employment Commission. She was a friend of
the family who knew me better than I knew
myself. "Hey Tim", she said with both corners of
her mouth almost touching her ears, "what are
you doing here? -- I know you didn't quit your
job at the hospital." "No ma'am," I stated.
"Actually, that's my intention, but first I want to
see if you can help me find a better job."
Excitedly she then stated, "A better job! Are you
crazy?" I had to calm her down before she would
have gotten the other people around us into our
conversation. "Don't you realize how lucky you
are to be working among doctors and nurses?" I

14

replied, "yes" and then I embarrassingly told her about the four forty-five an hour salary that I was earning. She sat there motionless and I could tell that she didn't believe me until I reached into my wallet and pulled out an old payroll stub that I always kept on me. It was my largest paycheck ever, eighty regular and two overtime hours worth of pay and net pay equaled two-hundred and ninety eight dollars and twenty-seven cents. After seeing and understanding why I wanted a better job, she turned towards her desk and began pressing buttons on her computer. I assumed she would come up with a large number of job listings for a stout energetic young man who all of a sudden had something meaningful in life to work for. "Well Tim, there are a few jobs here but most of them don't pay over five dollars an hour and the ones that do pay a bit more are hundreds of miles away from here." She then paused, still looking at her computer screen, and said, "Wait a minute, here's something". I glanced at her screen and saw the State of Texas symbol on it. I then saw people in Uniforms with what appeared to be a prison in the background. "Why don't you try to become a correctional officer? It 80%says here you have to be at least eighteen years old, no criminal record and have at least a high school diploma or G.E.D.!" I looked at her as if she was speaking another language, and said, "Are you nuts -- a correctional officer in the state penitentiary?" She continued, "Wait, wait this job may not be that bad, and besides, it pays triple of what you're earning now! If you are interested, it says here that there is a six-week training course, and after that, you will be assigned to work at a prison that you choose, and it just so happens, there's one just a few miles away from here." I said to her that I would return on a later day if I decided to pursue that job. Realizing that neither time, nor money, was on my side, I returned the next day to apply. I am over the age of eighteen, and I had never been into any trouble with the law. I took a pretest to determine if I could be eligible to get into a paid training academy, and passed with flying colors. I was all set, and was informed by Ms. Savoic to await the training academy. While waiting on the training academy to begin, all I could think about was myself, one hundred and thirty pounds, friendly, working around those murderers robbers, rapists... "Does life really have to be this hard?"

# II

# REVEALING MY PLANS

Friday evening a couple of my buddies, Scooby and Daryl, decided that they were in the mood to play some basketball.  Since I was already off from work, and my girlfriend Tausha was out of town visiting relatives, I had nothing else to do, so I joined them.  It was fun being around Scooby and Daryl, except when we got together to play basketball because I was better than them.  "Whoooaa man, don't loosen up the bolts that's holding the damn goal" said Daryl as I breezed past Scooby and threw down a thunderous two-handed slam-dunk.  "Damn Tim, you should have taken that scholarship to play college ball, you probably would be on you way to the pros", said Scooby. Then to my surprise, Daryl boldly stated, "Yeah and at least finding a place to stay and raising a child wouldn't be so hard."  I dropped the basketball and looked puzzled into his sweaty face.  "How did you know about Tausha being pregnant and me having to move out on my own?"  Man everybody knows -- Tausha is spreading the news like a wildfire."  Disappointed and astounded, I listened to him as he offered words of encouragement.  Other guys in the gym kept asking me to play another game of basketball but my nerves were shot, and all I wanted to do was sit and continue to let out sweat in the old wooden bleachers.

I knew that my friends were feeling a bit sorry for me, because obviously Tausha had already told them or else they would have not mentioned it. "Say fellas, in a couple of weeks I'm going to be attending a training academy." They asked eagerly, "Training academy? What for? I know you're not going into the army." I answered, "I'm going to become a Texas department of criminal justice prison guard!" They looked at each other, and then after a short pause, the laughter came. "Tim, how in the hell are you going to be a prison guard? You don't even weigh more than the night stick that you will probably be toting," stated Daryl while holding his stomach because he was laughing so hard! And Scooby was also laughing to the point where he was crying. I became furious at them because I thought they would support me. I stormed out the gym and never looked back. As a matter of fact, I decided not to mingle with these two anymore.

My coworkers at the hospital were more supportive of my decision to become a correctional officer. They knew that I was not earning nearly my worth.  They asked the same type of questions that everyone else was asking (about my size), however, they were just making sure that I knew what I was getting myself into. During the last week of my days employed at the hospital, up until the last day, I got many presents, good luck cards and even a going away party.  Doctors whom I did not even have scheduled surgeries at the hospital that day even visited me to wish me well and say goodbye.  I was extremely excited and scared because I was making a career transition and a lifelong decision.

# III

# LEARNING MY NEW CAREER

Three hours out of the barbershop, sporting a schoolboy type haircut, wearing a polo-type shirt neatly tucked into my well-starched slacks, with a backpack (filled with new notebook paper, pens and other supplies) over my shoulder, I was ready for training.  I was excited because this reminded me so much of my grade school days.  Yeah, today was the first day of the Texas Department of Criminal Justice Pre-Service Training Academy.  When I arrived, I was shocked to see how many other people were interested in this job.  I also noted the fact that I wasn't the only thin guy in the academy.  There were also females.  I didn't think that there would be any females interested in becoming a prison guard.

The instructor came into class and introduced himself as Sergeant Johnson, which was the next rank above Correctional Officer, and wasted little time getting started.  He explained to us that we had a lot of policies and procedures to learn about in only a six-week period.  He started out by explaining to us the benefit packages that T.D.C. Offered to their employees.  Of course he talked about the pay, which in the geographical area ranked about fourth. Sergeant Johnson explained to us that there are hundreds of rules and guidelines for the inmates to follow and also for the officers to follow. Some of the rules for officers to follow that he pointed out as being vital to keeping our jobs, were to not bring contraband into the prison, not to have or develop sexual/personal relationships with the inmates, and the most common (and frequently violated) was not following the "use of force" guidelines. Anytime that an officer came into physical contact with an inmate, no matter how minor, it had to be reported in writing as a use of force, and using force had to be justified. The inmate had to be posing a threat to the immediate safety of another individual. Whenever an inmate is resisting, an officer shall do whatever possible to gain control of that inmate. When the inmate calms down and is not resisting, that officer shall no longer use force, as the inmate is complying with all orders. Sergeant Johnson pointed out that countless officers have lost their jobs due to their behaviors. There were many guidelines we had to become familiar with, and it seemed impossible to learn all of them in such a short period of time. Everything was appealing to me except for the very last thing, which made me nervous -- we had to successfully pass the course, which consisted of a physical as well as a written test. After weeks of book assignments over policies and procedures, group assignments, and doing various physical exercises, we were given a date to take our final exam. This test consisted of one hundred and fifty questions dealing with math, reading, English, and writing. We were also notified that the test would be timed. The test did not really bother me, because all throughout grade school I was given plenty of tests, some of which were timed, some not. Whatever the case was, I usually passed with flying colors. The test day came, and I not only passed it, but passed it getting ninety-six percent of the questions correct and doing so in about half the time it took the average person to complete it! The next obstacle in our way was the physical test - and it was this part that made me nervous. The test consisted of running one mile within ten minutes, dragging a two hundred pound dummy thirty yards, and reciting our social security number after taking a deep breath of tear gas. Finally, for those of us who passed the final exam, and the physical test, we had to qualify on the shooting range by shooting a target from various distances, using a 357 revolver, an AK-47 and a shotgun. This part puzzled me because there are absolutely no guns inside any prison in the entire state. Inside the prison unit we will be armed only with a nightstick and a walkie-talkie if we were lucky. These events took place over a three-day period, and out of the sixty-three trainees, only twenty-seven of us successfully completed everything.

# IV

# ON THE JOB TRAINING

I awoke at six o'clock in the morning and I had no idea that today would mark the beginning of a series of challenges, lessons, rendezvous, etc., in my life. To most people, March 1, 1995 was just another day, but for me, this was the first day of my new career. Seven forty-five a.m. I arrived in the parking lot of the Maximum Security Prison unit in a city in southeast Texas. This prison housed approximately three thousand convicted felons, some for crimes ranging from petty theft, all the way up to capital murder. The sentences were anywhere from one day to forever. I stood in the parking lot with a million thoughts going through my head. Even though I knew what kind of people were behind those brick walls and those razor barbed-wire fences, I knew that they were not going to come out and give me a warm welcome.

As the other on the job trainees showed up, we all began talking and sharing our ideas with each other. As we conversed, our fears melted away, because we were talking about how we will stick together and help each other out. We realized that we all had the same fears, and thoughts, but we knew that we had bright futures and opportunities ahead.

It was eight o'clock straight up, and out of the front door of the entrance to the prison came a man who stood about six foot three inches tall. He was clean cut and had no facial expression whatsoever. His suit was a perfect fit and his shoes were shiny like a new silver dime. We all stood with one hundred percent of our attention focused on this man, because he seemingly was a man in power -- and indeed he was. He was the head Warden. He cracked a smile and stated, "Welcome aboard C.O.'s, it's good to have you all joining our staff. Let's go inside." As we followed him inside the perimeter fence, my heart began to beat like a bass drum in a parade. I didn't know if I was excited or scared at that moment, but I was extremely shaken when the fence slammed shut after the last person had entered.

The warden took us to a room where he and several supervisors talked to us about prison life, and our job descriptions. Some of them told stories about their own misfortunes, which discouraged us, while other supervisors told us things that encouraged us. Right at that moment, I realized there was conflict among the supervisors. A Lieutenant, who is one rank above a Sergeant, stood in front of us and started telling us to watch out for other supervisors and officers, because if they didn't like you for whatever reason, they would try to "roll" you, which meant get you fired or force you to quit. Another supervisor told us that he could care less what went on, all he wanted to do was show his face for eight hours and go home. I was stunned to hear such negativity. In the academy, the instructors told us that we would be like family, but then after hearing these things from the horse's mouth, I began to wonder what type of family he was referring to.

After all the pep talks were over, it was time to tour the unit. This was the moment that I, and all the other new officers, waited for. We stood at a tall steel door that had the words, "Absolutely no civilians past this point" on it – as we anxiously waited for it to open. As we walked through the entrance, we could not help but notice the way we were being stared at by inmates and officers. My first thought was to stare back at everyone to make them think I was a hard core brutal type person in an officer's uniform, but I didn't. I just kept walking with the group. Sergeant Johnson was our tour guide, and the first place we went to was a place called Administrative Segregation. This was a place described by some officers as the hardest place inside the prison. Most inmates here are hard-core -- that is why they are isolated from the rest of the prison inmate population. We then went to the Medical Department where we met with doctors and nurses who provided care to the inmates. The most interesting place we toured was the Officer's Dining Room, or O.D.R. This was set up like a restaurant where inmates waited on officers and just like a buffet at an outside restaurant we ate all the food we wanted. Difference was it was free! The place that scared me was General Population. All the inmates were walking freely and on many cell blocks there was only one officer to approximately one hundred inmates. All the buildings had numbers and their own colors. The one that stood out the most was Eight Building. This building was designed for hard-core General Population inmates who were frequent rule violators. There was riot gear behind a caged in fence, video cameras, and first aid kits everywhere. Eight Building was not the place I wanted to be! One of the more noticeable things I saw were that for every one white inmate, there were about sixteen black inmates. There also were the drag queens -- I always saw that type of stuff in the movies, but to see a man dress, walk, and talk, thinking he is a woman in real life was hilarious.

 We met a lot of other supervisors and we saw hundreds more inmates. We toured places like the maintenance department, the laundry department, the kitchen, and of course, more cell blocks. It was five o'clock and almost time to go home for the day. Thinking about how we toured the unit, we all had on our minds what shifts and departments we would soon be assigned. Almost every single one of us wanted to work the day shift, in the seemingly easiest department, but we knew when it came to that decision, we were powerless. It was strictly up to the personnel department. There were rumors floating around that usually when new officers, or "new boots," are touring the unit, supervisors in different departments will try to "hand pick" the officers that stood out. Most of the time, the one's who stood out were stocky-built guys. If the rumor had any truth to it, I did not have to worry about being hand picked. Most of us talked about the advantages, and disadvantages, of working in different departments. We all agreed that the entire place was dangerous, especially the kitchen, because there were usually only four officers back there, with about one hundred inmate-workers, and lots of butcher knives lying around for them to use. The laundry department was equally as bad because there were only two officers, with about fifty inmate-workers and about thirty steam irons in the place. In general population there was an A-side and a B-side, each side housing about twelve hundred inmates -- only difference was B-side housed the more younger, violent inmates, who were habitual rule violators. A-side housed the older aged inmates who usually caused no problems and most of the time followed the rules, but just like B-side, each cell block had only one officer on duty to about one-hundred and forty inmates. Nowhere in this place seemed to be exempt from danger, so I just waited to see which card I would be dealt.

I could not wait to see my friends, Daryl and Scooby, whom I started talking to again, to tell them about all the things that I observed that day, the scary stuff and the interesting stuff. The inmates do everything -- cook, clean, everything but count themselves and they seemed disciplined too, at least at that moment. Five fifteen and it was time to get our shift assignments or permanent schedule.  I was

handed and envelope and I opened and read.
Officer Timothy Hampton third shift
Administrative segregation.

# V

# Administrative segregation

Administrative segregation better know as "ad-seg" is considered the most dangerous place inside of any maximum-security prison unit. There were approximately five hundred or so inmates assigned to Ad-seg on the Unit. Each inmate housed alone in an eight by ten foot cell. The reason why these inmates are confined here is because they are down right violent. They have a prison history of staff assaults or some kind of escape history. The rules for these inmates are far more restrictive than those that apply to General population inmates. The main rule that I was comfortable with was the one that stated each inmate shall be confined to his cell for a period of twenty-three hours a day. With one hour being optional to the inmate on whether or not he wishes to be escorted (in handcuffs) by officers to a secured dayroom area with a pull up exercise bar and a television as a form of recreation. I also was comfortable with the fact that I was assigned to the third shift which meant my work hours are from ten o'clock at night till six o'clock the next morning, and the majority of the inmates are normally asleep during this time.

My first few weeks working inside of ad-seg was

a learning experience.   One thing that I learned was that it was hard to fend off my sleepiness. Another thing I learned was that these inmates here seem to have no track of time, so they tend to stay awake all night long to harass the officers on duty, read their literature, or most of the time to argue with other inmates about any and everything.  By me being a new officer, I paid full attention to them -- not realizing they were just trying to figure me out to see where I stood.  The hardest thing I had to deal with was the fact I was being talked to and about like a dog.  I thought these inmates would respect me because I was indeed an officer, but I thought wrong.  I often found myself in front of a cell having a shouting match with an inmate and almost every time the subject was about me being an "Uncle Tom", or about me oppressing all the black inmates in prison because I was so called "down with the white man's plan."  I found myself being caught up in an argument that I didn't start.  Every single night I found it hard to accept the vulgar and obnoxious remarks that were made towards me -- ninety nine percent of the time by a black inmate.  I can't remember one single morning that I did not need to take headache medicine at the end of my shift.

This quickly caused me to have a strong dislike and lack of concern about inmates and their issues. I often heard other officers talking down on inmates and telling their own versions of how inmates did not bother them. One officer told me that he used to pull the fire hose from the closet and spray water through the cell door and into an inmate's cell if they pissed him off. Another officer stated that one night he and about six more officers had woke an inmate up out of his sleep by going into his cell at two in the morning and beating the crap out of him. This was a common practice for officers to get together when they are bored and tell their stories of how they mistreated the inmates, to see who can describe their most brutal experience. I asked a couple of officers why is it that when they work the cell blocks, the inmates don't even speak or look at them, yet when other officers work the same cell block, the inmates are like wild animals? One of the officers looked at me while removing tobacco chew from his mouth and said, "those bastards know that if they mess with me, I'll beat the hell out of them." I was extremely startled by the officer's statement because we were taught in the academy to refrain at all costs from putting our hands on inmates for such reasons, and I didn't want to believe him. One night, I was assigned to work with this one particular officer, and an inmate started yelling and accusing him of urinating in the coffee that we served them at breakfast time. I just stood there and thought about the inmate's allegations for a second and found it strange that before we started serving breakfast, the officer had sent me untraditionally off the cell block to get him some paperwork, but I just stood there thinking, I was not gone long enough for the officer to pull such a stunt – – or was I ? The inmate cursed the officer and told him that he was a punk and at that moment the officer grabbed his radio and requested that three officers be sent over to the cell block. I didn't know what was about to happen, but I eagerly anticipated. When the other three officers arrived with the sergeant, the sergeant huddled the officers away from me and then instructed me to go and retrieve a still photo camera, which was located away from the cell block. I then rushed to the unit's central control room, retrieved the camera, and about four minutes later when I returned to the cell block, my eyes almost popped out of my head because of what I saw. Two officers holding down that very same argumentative inmate on the concrete floor covered from head to toe in his own blood. The third officer was holding his legs, which were in leg restraints, down, and the officer I was working with was filming the incident with a video camera recorder. I looked at the supervisor and asked what was going on. He said to me that when I went to get the still photograph camera, the inmate kicked open his door and tried to attack him and the other officers. I stood there puzzled because some of the inmate's blood was inside the cell all the way to his back wall, and there was no blood in front of the cell. I bought the story because I was new and this was, of course, the penitentiary. On my way home that morning, I began thinking to myself that I need to become harder on the inmates. I need to write more disciplinary infraction on them for any little thing they did wrong or maybe for nothing at all. I felt the need to act more like the officers who were involved in that altercation this morning. Then it hit me -- I came to realize that they justified an unnecessary use of force. I'm no dummy, but because I didn't see it, it was my word against three officers and a supervisor; besides, I was once told by an officer that if I were to snitch on another officer, I would get "rolled." The more I worked around my coworkers and inmates, the more I learned. I soon developed a plan that I was comfortable with. It was simple. Give respect to all officers and expect respect in return. If the inmates don't give respect to me, I ignore them. I applied this to inmates and officers, because after a while, I found out that officers can be more cruel to each other than to inmates. Half of my supervisors I gave respect to. The other half I tried to avoid because they respected no one, not even their officers, who put up with a lot to make his or her job easier. I also came up with a disturbing theory. Most of these white supervisors are prejudice towards blacks. My theory was supported by the fact that there were few black officers being promoted to supervisory positions, fewer black officers being allowed to have vacations, and fewer black officers being assigned to less stressful duty posts throughout the prison unit. An incident took place once that also supported my theory. A white inmate told me that he was a member of the Klu Klux Klan and that he was going to "kill me and all the rest of my nigger buddies" when he got out of prison. I wrote a disciplinary offense report, charging him with a level one, code four: threatening an officer, which is a serious offense in prison, especially when dealing with a human being's life. I turned the report over to my supervisor, who was white, and as he read over it he giggled and stated to me that he would take care of it. I never heard about my report again. I was upset because I had written the same offense report on two separate inmates in that past who were black, and they received harsh penalties instantly. I didn't question anyone about this incident, because all the supervisors had a way of justifying everything they did. Some of my fellow officers were friends with the supervisors -- this is not a problem, but it became a problem to me when the friendship was obvious at work. These were the officers that I demanded respect from because they felt since they were fishing partners with the supervisor they could talk to everyone any kind of way. I also learned that those who say too much end up not being around (fired). I took this to heart because one of my biggest fears was being fired, especially if I was only doing what was right. That is why I and so many other officers often kept quiet. I realized that I needed to somehow get reassigned to another department, so I wrote a letter to the personnel department and requested a change.

On August 21, 1995, I got a letter that stated effective September 1, 1995, I would be promoted to a correctional officer III, which is the highest correctional officer rank. The letter also stated that I would be allowed to work the morning shift -- six o'clock in the morning until two o'clock in the afternoon. I was thrilled because I was getting away from the nighttime shift and I would not have to fight my sleep anymore. However I was not thrilled at the fact that I was going to be reassigned to work in the B-side General Population area of the prison. My fears then returned, because B-side of General Population consisted of about twelve hundred inmates who were either just getting out of Ad-seg or on their way to Ad-seg, and most disturbing was the fact that they were not confined to their cells twenty three hours a day. As a matter of fact, during the hours I will be there, they would not be inside their cells at all, but inside a large day room area where I would be walking shoulder to shoulder with them, armed only with a night stick. I had to mentally prepare myself because I knew I was in for a whole new ball game. The shouting matches I often get into with the inmates will be face-to-face, instead of having bars between us. I also was fearing reuniting with several of the inmates who I had altercations with in Ad-seg. I could not avoid going to General Population and I could not afford to quit my job, so I just prepared to take the responsibility head on and hope for the best.

# VI

# PRESSURE FOR CORRUPTION

September 1, 1995 marked my sixth month as a T.D.C. officer. The brave soul I was six months ago until now -- is all of a sudden a cowardly lion. The first day of my new shift, while sitting in an early morning shift meeting, I gazed around the room and saw about forty other officers conversing with each other. Most of these officers have been in the system for a couple of years or more. Suddenly, everyone became quiet because two of our supervisors walked in.

"What's up people?" stated a tall stocky built black man, who to me looked like he just left the local disco club. He introduced himself as Sergeant Gilbeaux. He started telling us about our call-in sick procedures and stated that it was becoming a big problem. My thoughts were that either the officers who call in sick a lot are scared to come to work, or simply don't have respect for this man who obviously does not have respect for himself, by the way he talks and carries himself -- totally unprofessional.

After Sergeant "Pretty Boy" (what I called him) finished giving us a meaningless speech, everyone who was cat napping awoke and focused their attention on the other supervisor, who was a Sergeant also. He was a short baldheaded white guy who walked and talked like he just got out of the military. His lecture was a bit more sensible, however, far more disturbing. He basically stated to us not to take any "shit" from an inmate. Furthermore, he told us that if we were to get into a physical altercation with an inmate, by the time he gets to the scene, he "better see blood", and not the officer's blood either. I guess that he knew I was nervous because he looked at me directly in the face as he was addressing the shift and stated, "If you are scared, you don't need to be here." This offended me and also made me very afraid because I felt like I was being put into a position where I had to kick ass or get fired.

When shift meeting was over, I went to my assigned duty post: Eight Building C-block – which was at that moment lock-down due to a huge gang fight earlier in the week. Of the one hundred and thirty inmates there, I only remembered one from Ad-seg and he and I did not have any previous altercations. However, he did make his fellow inmates aware that I had a habit of writing disciplinary offenses, but they didn't seem to care.

The officer I was working with was a real nice

gentleman.  He was a short-thickly built middle-aged white man who enjoyed talking. This officer was a person I really enjoyed working with and I wished that I could be his partner everyday.  As we sat in the control picket, he started telling me about each and every correctional officer on our shift.  The more I listened to him, the more I began to think I was in a soap opera.  He told me that a lot of the officers, not only on our shift, but throughout the entire unit, tended to sleep with each other.  Also that Sergeant Gilbeaux (I referred to him as Sergeant Pretty Boy) did not care what any male officers did while at work as long as they didn't try to mingle with female officers, because he was very jealous and felt every woman on the unit belonged to him.  It was also revealed to me that Sergeant Gilbeaux did not get along with Sergeant Fitzgerald (the other sergeant) for work and personal reasons. He went on to tell me about officer survival of the inmates, but I was trapped mentally whether or not I should try to survive from my own two supervisors.

# VII

# THE CHANGE

Under enormous pressure, I felt that I had to prove to my supervisors that I deserved to remain an employee for the Texas Department of Criminal Justice. The only thing that was on my mind was how much Sergeant Fitzgerald stressed making inmates lose blood by violence, and that if we took too much lip from these inmates, we didn't need to be working here. I did some heavy thinking and realized this was by far the best job that I ever had. Besides, I didn't want to do, nor *not* do, anything to jeopardize it. There were often times when inmates would ask questions -- most of the time they were legitimate questions -- but I tried my best to give stupid answers and sometimes I gave no answers at all. For example, one inmate asked me what time his cell block would be allowed to go and eat chow. Instead of me answering, twelve o'clock noon, I would say "whenever I feel like letting you all go, now get the hell away from me." This would make me feel like it was the way for me to win respect from my supervisors. There were also lots of times when inmates did not like me giving them stupid answers to their questions and I would get into a shouting match with them. Most of the time I was confident that I would win the argument, because I was wearing an officer's uniform and because my supervisors ensured me that I was always right, even when I'm wrong.

One and zero, two and zero, three and zero, four and zero, before I realized it I was seven and zero. These numbers represent my major uses of force, or what I called my Penitentiary fights with inmates' win-loss record. These inmates went beyond shouting matches -- they ended up getting physical with me. A couple of these incidents were one-on-one, but I always had help either already there or just seconds away. Almost every single time I was involved in a major use of force, my supervisor would huddle everyone together and tell us what to write on our incident reports. There was once an incident where my supervisor informed me that I needed to "take care of a certain inmate". Because my reputation of an inmate ass-kicker was so wide spread, everyone looked upon me to initiate the "dirty work". My head was so pumped up with nonsense, until I actually started believing that I was invincible. I felt like I was above other officers, I felt like I was above T.D.C. rules and regulations, I felt like I was above all inmates, and I sometimes felt I was above life itself. I found myself focusing more on T.D.C and the prison unit than on my own family, and things far more important in life. It made me feel good to see my supervisors smiling every time I went around them. It made me feel like a "big man" to walk down a long hallway and harass inmates for absolutely no reason at all, and go back and brag about it to my sergeants. On several occasions I was invited to start fights with inmates, and sometimes I had already written the paperwork justifying the use of force, before I actually got involved in it. Whenever I met up with officers who were "down with me", or me down with them, we went to inmates' cells and destroyed things that were valuable to them, such as their family photos, certificates they may have earned while in prison, and sometimes we even consumed their commissary items. Most of these inmates we did these things to were targeted because they had pissed someone off, usually a female officer, and she put the order in. Other inmates sometimes put themselves in harms way by playing with officers, or arguing with us. One situation took place where this one particular inmate had just reminded the sergeant of how bad his haircut had looked. Sarge tried to counter with wise cracks of his own in the shouting match with the inmates, but found himself becoming more and more embarrassed as dozens of inmates laughed at what was being said about him. "Officer Hampton," said the sergeant, "how about escorting this inmate back to his cell -- and while escorting him in handcuffs, how about if he slips and hits the concrete sidewalk - hey, shit happens" So I ordered the inmate to stand up, submit to handcuffs, and exit the chow hall as my supervisor whispered to me "you know, shit happens." I then had a feeling of what kind of shit he was talking about and as we were away from all the other offenders and alone on the sidewalk... You know, shit happened.

Because I made all of my major uses of forces justifiable, my supervisor had an easy time with my incident reports, and often bragged on me to other supervisors through out the prison. This made me feel proud because I knew that my supervisors like me. Hell, all I had to do was whip an inmate here and there, complete the proper paperwork, and my days working for that state were unnumbered. Before too long, I was asked by a higher department head to try and promote to supervisor because to them I was "setting the tone for other officers". I was even

taken off the cell blocks and given a work squad
of approximately one hundred inmates to
oversee. My supervisor told me to just " work
the dog shit out of those bastards" and the
squad was mine forever!

The broom and shower squad, made up of
approximately one hundred inmates, was my
new assignment. My job was to take about
twenty of them at a time and scrub floors, walls,
etc., from six o'clock in the morning until two
o'clock in the afternoon.

On a daily basis I literally worked these inmates
until their bodies were soaked in sweat. My
power hungry egotistical mind often came up

with outrageous assignments such as cleaning dirt from sidewalk cracks with a toothbrush, or cleaning hundreds of windows – allowing each individual to use only a single cotton ball.

Every time my supervisor walked by and saw what I had going on, he smiled like he didn't have a care in the world.

One day while overseeing my workers, the unit's safety supervisor approached me and asked if he could see my updated safety training roster. I told him that I didn't know what he was talking about. He explained to me that every thirty days my inmate workers had to be given safety training, meaning read safety rules and going over different chemicals that we work with and so on. I had only two days before I would be found in violation and could face disciplinary for not giving proper safely training to the inmates I worked.

I confronted my supervisor about the dilemma that I was suddenly in, and he responded by saying "That's your responsibility." Immediately, I felt betrayed because all of a sudden my ass is on the line and all the supervisors I looked up to were suddenly unconcerned. I didn't let the situation get the best of me, so I went to the unit's safety supply office and retrieved as many safety manuals as I could find. I came out of the office with several safety topics and a roster that all my workers could sign. I then made an announcement for all broom and shower squad workers to report to the gymnasium the following morning. The next morning, I walked into the gymnasium where about only half of my workers showed up. I made the announcement that whoever was not present would be written up for refusing to report to work. I then stood there for a minute (not knowing how to conduct a safety meeting), overlooked the guys who had all their attention focused on me, and began reading rules and tips from the safety manual. During my presentation I often noticed that there was one inmate who was coaching me as I spoke. Then a strange twist occurred. The inmate who was coaching me, who the other inmates referred to as "Chicago," approached me and asked if he could demonstrate some of the rules while I read over them. Inmate Chicago told me that I needed to give examples of safety rules as I read them, like the proper way to put on and remove rubber gloves. I was puzzled because I could not figure out why the inmates I worked like slaves were so willing to help me. When I finished the meeting, I asked inmate

Chicago why he and the other inmates were so willing to help me even though I treatec them like dogs? He stated "Hamp, we can see it in your eyes, you are not a bad person, you just let these other officers and crooked supervisors get the best of you." Inmate Chicago went on to tell me that he had been locked up years for murder and that he had seen a lot of officers like myself. He told me that I needed to be myself. His very first example was the fact that no one was willing to help me with my safety meeting. I found myself listening to Chicago and also the other inmates whom I was around.

They all encouraged me to become a more positive person, and not let the corrupters in the T.D.C. (Officers and inmates) corrupt me. I took those things to heart and I came to a decision. I needed to win respect from these inmates as a person first and then as an officer. I needed a starting point, so I started in society and then at work. I asked my supervisors to return my duty to the cell block were it all began. Once there, an incident took place that showed me that no matter how neatly starched and ironed my uniform was, no matter how much my supervisors liked me, or no matter how many officers liked me, I was not immune to the violence that sometimes occurred behind the prison wall.

 While assigned to work on Eight building's desk, I observed two inmates involved in a verbal confrontation on the recreation yard. One was a black inmate, and the other inmate was a Mexican. The argument quickly led to a fist fight, and me, not making a wise decision, ran out onto the recreation yard without my night stick nor a radio. I guess I was so caught-up into being the superman of the penitentiary, until I got complacent. While I ran toward the two inmates who were fighting, I heard the door slam behind me. I glanced back and saw a white inmate barricade the door with his body, preventing anyone from exiting the yard, including myself. As I ran toward the fight I also noticed that several of the inmates who were already out there ran towards different areas of the yard and retrieved homemade knives or what might be know to many as prison shanks. "Oh shit!" I thought, as I realized I was in the middle of a riot. So instead of running toward any one area, I ran in circles and prayed. I heard the siren go off to alert other officers around that there was indeed a riot. That gave me little hope because I now realized that help was on the way. Before the other officers got to the scene I was grabbed and thrown to the ground by an inmate who I didn't see. I just knew I was about to be stabbed to death or kicked and beaten because I was "free game". Instead of knives being poked inside me or kicks and punches landing on me, a giant mattress that is used to prevent someone from running into the brick wall landed on me. At that time I was so in shock that I passed out. When I came to, there were other officers around me laughing saying, "I see you hiding under that mattress." I was puzzled for a second, but happy I was not injured. I then realized that an inmate had saved me from getting injured or possibly killed. All I could think about was why an inmate cared about an officer, especially an officer who treated them like crap. Whatever the reason -- it made me think.

# VIII

# TARGETING A CHANGED PERSON

As today got started, I felt strange feelings in my gut. This was the very next morning after I requested to my supervisor that I be assigned to work the minimum-security cell blocks. My supervisors, who were usually excited to see me every morning, all of the sudden had little to say to me. The group of officers who encouraged me and sometimes asked for advice from me did not save me a seat in the officer's dining room where we often had breakfast together before shift meeting. And finally, to condone my gut feeling, I was not assigned to work the hard-core cell blocks which housed nearly all of the inmates who had worked for me. Instead, I was assigned to work the outside guard tower where I had no contact with inmates nor officers. Eight long hours alone overlooking the entire prison unit. At first, I was bitter. But I looked on the bright side -- I will no longer have to deal with the pressure of beating up on inmates just to satisfy my superiors and uphold, what I now realized, to be a negative reputation.

Five working days had passed and I was placed back inside the perimeter fence. I was assigned to work around the minimum custody classified inmates. Mr. Petry was always assigned to work around the minimum custody inmates because he was labeled "inmate friendly". I knew this from being around the supervisors a lot, however, Mr. Petry did not. I also received this message that was sent to me through my assignments from my supervisors - it read: "Since you're friendly now, you can work with officers such as Mr. Petry." One day while sitting in the day room discussing biblical versus with several inmates, Mr. Petry approached me and asked me if he could talk to me alone. I excused myself from the table among the inmates whom I now looked at as my brothers, and walked across the day room to a quiet area of the wing. Mr. Petry immediately began telling me how he had been observing me, and the things that were going on with me. He told me that he was proud of me for finally trying to use my head instead of a nightstick. We went on and talked about some of the situations that were taking place throughout the prison unit. He warned me that I was now on my own meaning any decision that I would make from here on out I would have to live and deal with. As we talked over an hour and a half, I felt so good inside. I felt like a person. Mr. Petry had helped me restore pride and dignity within myself -- I felt a feeling of true pride and self-respect -- and he did it without implicating violence. I felt embarrassed because it's been a couple of years now and I truly regret all the wrong doings that I have witnessed and done, not only to convicted felons, but people in general. I had an overwhelming confidence that if I would have met Mr. Petry in the very beginning of my job, it would not have been like this. I realized it's all in a plan. Whenever new officers come in, expose them to corruption and scare them into thinking that it is the only way to keep their jobs and, most importantly, keep officers like Mr. Petry away from them.

Crying on the inside, although my face showed mixed emotions, I boldly gave Mr. Petry a hug and asked him to pray for me, even while we were in the view of many inmates. Mr. Petry did not even hesitate and laid his hand on my head and began praying for me.

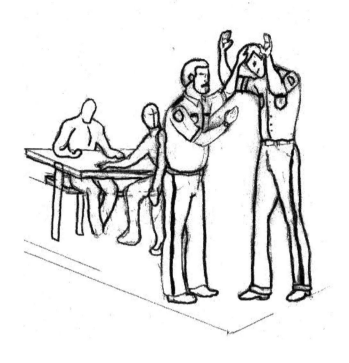

Several weeks passed by and I honestly started to feel like I was becoming a better person each day. I found myself reading the bible more, paying more attention to inmate's issues, and even participating in community activities outside of work. Soon, every single day at work, inmates who walked by greeted me with a huge smile and told me that he appreciated how I took time out to help them. My coworkers, the good ones of course, have silently chosen me as a role model in and out of the prison. I often got compliments from them on how I was taking care of my business.  Even a few supervisors had noticed the change in me and they praised me.

In the back of my mind I knew that things were going all too well. While working on a minimum custody wing, I was on the telephone with Officer Montgomery who was a veteran officer.  Officer Montgomery was working on the Eight Building close custody side.  As we talked, he suddenly exclaimed "oh shit Hampton, let me let you go, I see officers running to C-block -- there must be some kind of trouble going on."  I said, "OK", hung up the phone, and immediately started praying for the safety of my coworkers and the inmates who could possibly be in conflict right then.  A few minutes later, my telephone rang and Officer Hallow told me that Sergeant Shields wanted me to come over to Eight Building.  I was so concerned about everyone else safety, I honestly did not think I would be in any conflict. I saw officer Montgomery on my way to Eight Building, stopped him, and asked what happened.  He said that the other officers were about to beat up inmate Jones.  I said," well nothing happened right", and he said "no". When I arrived on Eight Building, it was quiet and it did not look like anything serious had happened. Sergeant Shields said that he wanted me to go onto C-block and look inside Forty-three cell and tell me how many inmates were inside. I thought this was strange because there were about five other officers near Sergeant Shields, and it was not time to count the inmates. Besides, I was assigned to work clear on the other side of the prison. I could not refuse his request, or else I would be facing disciplinary action, so I proceeded to C-block. Once inside the day room, I noticed that there were no other officers near -- but I went on ahead to carry out my duty. I approached forty-three cell, looked inside, and there were two inmates inside the cell sleeping. Before I could turn and walk away, forty-two cell had mysteriously opened and out came inmate Jones, mad as hell yelling "Oh, Hampton they sent you to beat me up.... well come on... I'll kick your ass!" I then pulled my nightstick and told inmate Jones to stop and walk back into his cell. He did so and I secured his door and said to him "Man I'm not here to fight you or anyone else. I was sent here by Sergeant Shields to..." I then stopped in the middle of my sentence and apologized to inmate Jones for any inconvenience. I then walked to the picket control officer and asked how did forty-two cell door get opened. The officer stated he thought I said to open it. To me, it was a bold statement from him because I didn't even look at him. Again I realized this was a plan "they" came up with to take me under. As I waited for the door to open so I could exit the block, I looked and saw Sergeant Shields and his crew looking at me seemingly to see if I had any wounds. Then they hurried and looked away. After I exited the block, I walked past Sergeant Shields and left the building. Immediately after that, he came out and repeatedly called my name to come back, but I kept walking. He shouted to me that he was going to write me an employee disciplinary offense. I was so furious that I turned toward him and stated, "Fuck you Sarge." I put my future in jeopardy by that remark because cursing a supervisor was grounds for dismissal. I walked all the way out the front gate and went home and wrote down what had happened. I stated that my supervisor knowingly and willingly put my physical safety in jeopardy by having a cell door opened while I was on the cell block alone.

The next day when I returned to work, Sergeant Shields had written me the disciplinary offense for insubordination towards a supervisor and cursing a supervisor. He gave it to his supervisor, a lieutenant. I then gave a copy of my written statement as to what happened to the lieutenant also, without Sergeant Shields knowing. Surprisingly, nothing happened to me. It just leaked out that my statement was stronger than the Sergeant's accusations and advice was given to him (by an unknown source) to forget about it or he'll end up getting disciplined. After that incident, I remembered that Mr. Petry had warned me that I was on my own and I had to make wiser decisions and cover myself. I knew that Sergeant Shields was going to retaliate against me in another way. Each department had various duty positions -- the most common position being a Rover Officer. The person assigned to this duty was responsible for counting inmates at designated count times, conducting random cell searches, conducting showers, and other various duties. The control officer was responsible for opening doors the rover requested, making or taking telephone calls (sometimes other departments call and request for inmates who may have appointments or be assigned to work there.) Most importantly, the control officer was a lifeline in case the rover was in need of backup. It was extremely important that the control officer watch the rover at all times. A gate officer was an absolute horrible position. If an officer was assigned to a gate, he was responsible for pat searching and randomly strip-searching every inmate that passed through. On each shift, there were an average of about six hundred inmates going through this process. Many officers who were assigned to a gate position were put there to be punished or harassed by the supervisor. When questioned about being assigned to the gate repeatedly, the most common answer supervisors came up with was," I could put you anywhere."

Policy-wise it was justifiable and okay. It was down right dirty and demoralizing to work an officer in that position more than three times a month, especially when there is an excess of one hundred officers assigned on shift. Some officers were on gate duty about ten times a month. A utility officer was a position designed for the leftover officers who were not assigned a duty position at all. This occurred usually when there was an overstaffed shift. Their duties were simple -- just help out where ever an officer may need help, such as cell blocks, control pickets, and gates. Most utility officers, however, took advantage of the "reward", helped no one, and hid the entire shift. Ironically, most officers being assigned a utility position were the same officers who get the same position day after day. Even though each correctional officer got paid the same according to their rank, there still was a difference in how some officers went home overworked and some went home full of energy. I was prepared to face many days as a gate officer and, sure enough, I was assigned to a gate about three times a week.

# IX

# SURVIVING THE GAME

Just like so many people in my community, as well as higher prison officials had warned me, inmates always tried to test me just to see how much I will let them get away with. Sometimes they were trying to eat twice in the chow hall, there are also times when they will try and sell or trade with other inmates their personal property. Depending on the mood the officer on that particular day, the inmate may or may not get by. The most common violation an inmate might try is asking an officer to bring him in something from the free world such as alcohol, tobacco, and even illegal narcotics. Sex is not to be excluded from these violations either. From my observation and personal experiences, I found that an inmate tries to establish a common bond between himself and the officer. One thing I learned even in the training academy is that when you are talking with an inmate, if he asks a lot of questions pertaining to your personal life, he is trying to "bait" you in or form a bond. For instance, a situation happened with me with this one particular inmate -- inmate Louis. He remembered my name in newspaper articles from when I played high school basketball. He would always call me "Officer

State Champ," and every time I heard this I cracked a smile. One day, I had a short talk with him. During our conversation, he asked me what position I played, how many points I averaged a game, and so on. I answered every single one of his questions and he obviously realized how much I loved basketball. He then went on to tell me that he was also a former high school basketball star who, before he was sent to prison, was on his way to college with a full scholarship -- and he talked about how much he loved the game. Everyday, from that point on, if he asked me for extra milk, I gave it to him. If he asked me to stay at recreation a little while longer (to get in a couple of extra jump shots) I allowed him to. I mean, how could I let someone who I felt was just like me not be allowed to live with a little better circumstances than T.D.C. allowed?

One day, this inmate's confidence was up I guess, and he called me over to his cell and started talking about playing basketball and remaining calm under pressure. He said all his statistics were up when he played calm, and his secret was "to smoke a cigarette before every game". Me, not realizing what was being plotted, continued to listen as the inmate lowered his head in shame and stated to me how much of his game had been lost. I began to feel sorry for him because I don't know what I would do with myself if my basketball skills faded just a little. Then I guess he saw the compassion on my face for him and he said, "Officer State Champ, if I only had a pack of cigarettes everything would be all right." At the same moment, Ms. Jones, the teacher from the education department, came over and said to him, "Congratulations, your test scores came back and you are ready to enroll in school at the high school level." As she reached into her briefcase to get some forms for the inmate to fill out, I curiously asked, "Why are you repeating high school?" Ms. Jones then looked at me and said, "Inmate Louis quit going to school when he was in the free world at age twelve." I stood there shocked and betrayed because all the days inmate Jones and I were talking, he was making up stories as he went along. He felt shame, because his cover was blown. So I did not pressure him and try to find out why he had chosen me. I did state to him, though, that I did not want him referring to me as "Officer State Champ" and I also let him know that I did not care to talk with him anymore.

Also, I realized that an inmate has twenty-four hours a day to think and figure out how he can get over on me. My problem was that I gave every inmate a chance to prove himself as a positive remorseful citizen. I also went out of my way and beyond my call of duty to see to it that an inmate was being properly treated, but too many times, I was labeled friendly and tried to be taken advantage of. I chose not to do anything for the inmates whom I found were guilty of these things. They labeled me "uncle tom" or "sell out." It seemed I could not please everyone, no matter how hard I tried.

# X

# THE PROMOTION ROADBLOCK

It seems like the problems and controversies that come along when you're talking about the penitentiary are never ending. At this point in my career, I really felt like I could make a difference. I never had so much confidence in a plan where I believed I could single-handedly make conditions better for myself, my coworkers, my supervisors, and for the three thousand inmates who lived in this penitentiary. My solutions were simple -- use more professionalism, which I deemed as a individual doing his or her job the right way to the best of his or her ability; also to use more common sense, or making sound decisions. I had to get into a position where I could be heard so I can put my plan into effect.

The sergeant of correctional officers was the first promotion on the T.D.C. Career ladder. A sergeant's responsibility is to ensure that all correctional officers are working together and being responsible for their actions. His duties included assigning correctional officers to various cell blocks and outside areas of the prison unit on a daily basis. The sergeant was also responsible for handling problems that officers might have with inmates. A sergeant is also someone who ensures that his correctional officers are showing a positive example to inmates, while they go through their rehabilitation process. Since I was already doing these things, and I had four years worth of experience, I felt that when the next sergeant of correctional officers' position became available, there could be no other person who was more fit then myself.

I decided to stop by the unit's personnel office, and to my delight I read that there would be an interview to promote a new sergeant in two weeks. I knew I had all the personal qualities of a sergeant -- I mean, I was professional and nearly all the inmates and fellow officers looked up to me. But I needed to polish up my skills when it came to policies and procedures. When I announced to my coworkers that I was pursuing a sergeant's position, they all responded with cheer and many of them agreed that the unit needed someone like me to be in such a position. My coworkers were so supportive of me that some of them gave me literature from the unit's promotion committee, which contained rules and guidelines dating back to when T.D.C. only had two prison units. I studied the material every night and I often paused to think about how I planned to treat and train the officers who I would be responsible for with pride, dignity, and respect -- something that we as correctional officers lack. Ever since announcing my plan, everyday I could see the excitement in everyone's eyes -- even the inmates and other supervisors. Everyone anxiously anticipated me becoming "Sergeant Hampton." Two days before I was scheduled to interview with the promotion committee, my coworkers gave me a surprise party in the O.D.R. I was thrilled and I deemed this day as a change for the better. About an hour into my party, my supervisor handed me a letter and shook my hand. I told him thanks and he smiled and walked away. Since all the material I had been receiving lately had been encouraging letters, I folded this one, placed it into my back pocket, and continued with the celebration.

I arrived home exhausted, covered from head to toe in sweat -- excited like a little boy who just received a brand new bicycle for Christmas! The only thing on my mind was to get in and out of the shower and get a good night's rest, because tomorrow was the eve of my promotional interview. As I stood at my dresser and gazed into my own eyes in the mirror, I emptied my pockets and thought about the steamy hot water that was awaiting me. On the dresser laid my keys, my pager, a peppermint, my wallet, and the note that Sergeant Fitzgerald had given to me. Everything was out of my pockets. As I took a seat on the end of the bed, I reached for the letter. I was curious to find out what my supervisor had written me because he almost never had anything verbal to say to me. I opened the envelope and unfolded the letter and it read: "To Officer Hampton, from the Internal Affairs Division. Officer Hampton, I am Lieutenant Walker with the prison unit internal affairs Department and it has been called to my attention that you were involved in a major use of force with an inmate and you may have been in violation." By this time, the sweat that had evaporated had all of a sudden returned, and my eyes were bulging from my head -- the whole time, not believing the words I was reading. The letter went on to explain that I was involved in a physical altercation with an inmate in September of 1995 and after reviewing my written statement there was conflict between my own statement and what another officer who was a witness had written. First, I am trying to figure out why four years later this incident is coming about? Secondly, I am trying to figure out which inmate this could have been and which officer wrote such a statement that was obviously against me. And finally, since I am under investigation, what kind of position would I be in as far as my interview in less than forty-eight hours? When I arrived at work the next morning my very first stop was at the internal affairs room. I knocked on the door and to my surprise Sergeant Fitzgerald had answered. When he saw it was me, he left, and I went inside and talked with Lieutenant Walker. "Officer Hampton, I didn't expect you to come so soon." He stated. "Well sir, I wanted to get this matter cleared up as soon as possible," I stated while handing him the letter that I had from him. He informed me that I was involved in a major use of force in 1995 and, according to my statement, the inmate had thrown a punch at me first. He allowed me to read my four year old statement and I gave it back to him and stated, "yes sir, this is exactly how it happened." He then opened another folder with the title Statement from Derreck Petry. I was totally in shock because this is the same Mr. Petry who often prays for me and encourages me. I was feeling extremely bitter towards Mr. Petry. Then I had remembered when this incident took place Mr. Petry was right there. He saw everything! Lieutenant Walker then boldly allowed me to read what Mr. Petry had written. I could not believe Mr. Petry's statement as I was reading it. He stated that: Officer Hampton was extremely aggressive during the altercation. Officer Hampton displayed excessive use of force. His statement also said that the inmate never attempted to strike me. His statement was signed and dated. This totally devastated me not only because I will not be allowed to attempt to promote to a supervisor but I felt Mr. Petry could have told me about this, and he should have never became friends with me. As I walked out of the internal affairs office, Lieutenant Walker reminded me that the entire major use of force would be reinvestigated and that I would not be allowed to attempt to promote until the investigation was complete.

As the day progressed, many of my coworkers as well as inmates questioned me about a rumor that they had heard pertaining to me withdrawing my name from the promotion list. All I could do was simply acknowledge the fact that I had. Once as a little boy my mother told me that life was full of disappointment. I never expected to be disappointed the way I am now. I had so much confidence and faith that I was going to become a supervisor, and basically this expectation was taken from me overnight.

On the day that the promotion committee was interviewing supervisor hopefuls, I showed my support by giving little hints of how to answer questions to the candidates. At one point, I started to cause some confusion because of the three officers who were interviewing for the position, two of them had been found in violation on several employee rules including major use of force violations and the other one was an officer who was a T.D.C. Officer for only six months and had been accused several times of bringing tobacco into the prison unit to give to inmates.

Many of my coworkers felt let down because they too had expected me to become a supervisor. I never bothered to explain to them why I withdrew my name from the interview because I did not want everyone to start disliking Mr. Petry.

The next morning at work, Mr. Petry rushed over to me and asked what my problem was and why I haven't been acting my normal cheerful self? I stared him directly between the eyes, like a bull before he charges red, then uncontrollably I began crying, asking "what do you mean Mr. Petry, why do you think I am not being myself? It is because of a statement you wrote against me on a use of force. That is why I did not interview for the sergeant position!" Mr. Petry looked at me with his mouth wide open and just watched as I walked away sobbing. Later that afternoon, I started getting phone calls from everyone on the unit. It seems Mr. Petry had informed a couple of people, who informed a couple more people of what I said to him that morning. I had let everyone know who had called me that day that I did not want to talk to anyone.

After work that day there were a lot of my coworkers waiting for me at my car. I could not tell them I did not feel like being bothered then because there were about thirty officers there, all who defended Mr. Petry and told me to cheer up and the truth would come out.

On the next morning Mr. Petry called me and asked me to meet him at the internal affairs office after work. I started to just skip the meeting, but I decided to join him. It's now two o'clock and I am waiting for Mr. Petry outside of the I. A. D. office, when he arrives shortly after. He tells me that he had previously spoken with

Lieutenant Walker who told him not to worry about the investigation. Mr. Petry said that this made him more suspicious and the fact that he would never write anything that would make someone look bad. We knocked on the door and were allowed to enter the office. Once inside, Mr. Petry did all the talking and he asked Lieutenant walker to allow him to see the statement he had written. "Well, well, well, this is a darn shame," stated Mr. Petry who then viscously slammed the statement on the desk and said, "This isn't even my hand writing!" And most surprisingly the statement was written on September 15th 1998 and the use of force took place on September 15th 1995! While Lieutenant Walker threw his hands up and proclaimed his innocence, I lowered my head in disgust. I was not disgusted because I was happy or the fact that I was no longer under investigation or because I missed out on a precious moment in my career. I was disgusted all due to a well planned, but poorly executed, conspiracy against me. The news about what Mr. Petry had found out shocked everyone throughout the unit. I am sure whoever was responsible for such a sleazy act was shocked too. However, no one bothered to come forth with an explanation. Seems like life is just not fair.  Every time I try to take a step forward, seems like I was pushed back two steps, not only in prison, but outside of the prison walls. What had happened to me was probably the worst thing since my mother had died back in 1988.  Chills ran through my body when I compared the scenarios.

The sneaky kid that I was never bothered to tell my mother about all the trouble that I used to get into.  I used to go into stores and steal candy or toys.  Sometimes both.  Whatever I used to get my hands on.  I used to fight at school constantly.  My mother was a single mother of four, she worked two jobs to raise me and my siblings, and did not deserve to get the heartaches that I caused, and the changes that I put her through.  Just like the way I used to treat inmates was the same way I had treated my mother.

November 3rd, 1988, my mother dropped me off to Lincoln High School where I was a freshman.  She had no idea that as soon as she drove off I would be doubling back, walking to alternative school.  Two days prior to today, I was again suspended from school for fighting and I didn't bother telling my mother.

On that morning, November 3, 1988, while

sitting in the one room hut completing lessons that my home school had sent for me to complete, I began to sit and just think about all the hardships that I cause my mother. I began searching for peace within myself and realized that I had to stop my wrongdoings. Besides, I was fifteen and had just entered high school. I peered around the room to see if anyone was watching me, and I began to pray. I began asking the lord Jesus Christ for forgiveness, for my sins, and for everything I had done to my mother. After about five minutes of prayers, I decided that after school I would come clean with my mother and explain to her that I was serving a suspension of five days for fighting at school. About ten minutes had passed and I'm feeling brand new. Principal Louis' voice came over the intercom, "Ms. Chucks." Ms. Chucks, who was the teacher in the room at that time, responded, "Yes." "Do you have Timothy Hampton in your class?" he asked as my heart raced and my blood pressure skyrocketed. "Yes I do," she responded. And Mr. Louis said, "send him to my office." As I proceeded to his office, all I could think about was that my mother had found out I was suspended, or the principal found out that was not my mother's signature on my suspension papers. When I arrived at the office, Mr. Louis told me to just have a seat. At the same time, an unknown woman's voice asked, "Is he here?" Mr. Louis said yes and she appeared and looked at me and frowned. I was extremely puzzled because minutes had went by and several adults came to the office and just looked at me.

Five more minutes passed and Mr. Louis told me my ride had arrived. At the time I did not know I was going anywhere. I walked outside and saw my grandmother and my aunt waiting for me. In my grandmother's car I did not say anything, I just got inside the car. Mr. Louis closed the door behind me and then put his hand on my head and said, "Son, let me explain something to you. A couple of hours ago your mother was driving her school bus and a ten year old boy had a gun onboard and shot your mother." I was stunned at what I was hearing because it was only a few moments ago that I decided to get my life together and show my mother what a wonderful person I could be and would become. All of a sudden that chance was taken away from me. As the chills continued to overwhelm my body, I could not believe how this is the second time I vowed to become better, yet when it is time for me to show it...

Being a correctional officer is probably one of the hardest careers that an individual can have. The hardest social standpoint in society is probably being a minority. Now take those two, combine them with being confused about adopting a decent religion, to serve Christ, dealing with the stress of "baby mama" drama, and trying to get by on the sixty-five percent of pay that I see each month after the government and attorney general "get theirs", and you have just walked a mile in my shoes! When most people listen to me talk about my past experiences, in and out of prison, they take the shoes off after only about a block.

One of the many lessons that I learned while working inside of prison is how to survive with little or no resources. About two years into my career, I had the resources to become a better officer and gain a better position behind that wall. However, it was stripped away from me. What no one can strip from me though is the peace of mind that I have and the knowledge. True enough, I won't be able to promote to become a supervisor for another two years, but believe me, I will be ready. If for some reason there are obstacles in my way, I will go over them. My most recent experiences did not at all damage my pride or self esteem. If anything, I used my experiences as a motivational tool. My next goal is to win over as many people as a can. I want everyone to know that Officer Hampton is one of the most prolific persons on the face of the earth. Not because of my misfortunes, but because I strive and go out of my way to help people in anyway I can.

Everyone has always known me for my wittiness. Sometimes people who I worked with would just want to come around me because they know I had something silly to say or do. Most of the time when I would be silly, I was just hiding hurt or wanted someone else to forget about his or her hurt for a minute.

Inside prison, being silly is not expected or tolerated except for when you are around people like yourself. Two of my best friends worked as correctional officers also. They were Officers Hines and Drum. We often got together and told jokes or just talked about each other. Whatever we decided to do we had fun doing it, and sometimes we joked with the inmates. This made us enjoy our job and I could tell that it made inmates feel comfortable around us. This was extremely important to me because establishing a bond with everyone was the first and major part of my plan.

Because of all the attention I was getting inside of the prison recently, and because of the big fuss that my coworkers made, I suddenly felt like I was a marked man. I felt someone was out to get me in a bad way. Jealousy and hate were the two feelings that I felt the most. I know it was coming after I decided to no longer beat up inmates, but I did not know what form it was coming in.

One day while assigned to work inside the prison's medical department, I was approached by an officer who was working the emergency room. He was a young white officer who had glanced at my nametag. "Are you Officer Hampton who works in general population?" he said. "Yes, I am," I responded, "Why do you ask?" The younger officer stated to me that he had heard all about me from inmates as well as other officers. He said to me that he would not mind being like me, then he quickly corrected himself, saying, "I mean I would not mind getting the respect from the inmates like you, but I do not want the criticism and attention that you get from certain officers and supervisors." In my response to him, I asked, "Are any of those officers or supervisors who criticized me showing a positive image in this penitentiary?" "As a matter of fact, they are not -- they are the ones who are always beating up inmates or not coming to work most of the time," stated the young officer. "My point exactly!" I said in a strong voice. I then asked him, "Why would you want to risk your physical safety and your job following a rambunctious group of officers and/or supervisors?" "You are right, officer Hampton, I see why many of these inmates respect you so highly, I am sorry if I offended you earlier." "You did not offend me, trust me people around here have done some pretty mean things towards me, so you have not done anything to me," I said. As we continued to talk, I asked the younger officer if he wanted to, he could hang out with me during or after work. I let him know that I understood if he did not want to hang with me during working hours, because he may get harassed by the same group of people who were against me. The younger officer smiled and said that he would be thrilled to hang out with me after work, particularly when I go and play basketball. He too remembered reading about some of my past high school heroics. I smiled as I realized I won the respect of yet another individual. As I walked away, the officer stated "Hey Hampton, be careful, man, I overheard the Sergeant talking to some officers last week and he was telling them to watch everything you did and try and get some dirt on you so the system can oust your ass." I put my hand on his shoulder and smiled and stated "Youngster, answer me this question. If Jesus Christ is for you, who can be against you?" Then I turned and walked away again. A Few days after this encounter, I was instructed to work inside of ad-seg because there was a shortage of officers. I had no problem with this, and if I did, it would not have mattered anyway. I was assigned to A-wing for the shift. While carrying out my duties, an inmate requested that I come to his cell. When I approached his cell, he motioned for me to come closer, obviously he had something top secret to tell me. As I eased closer to his cells door, he showed me a clipping of a newspaper article about three white men who were accused of dragging a black man to death using a pickup truck. He then pointed frantically towards the cell next to him and whispered, "that's him, let me out Hamp, let me whip his ass please". I then looked into the cell next door and sure enough, the white man inside resembled one of the men. Being optimistic, because I know several people can look alike and have the same names, I went to the control picket and asked the officer "is that one of the men who was accused of committing that horrible crime in a small town in Texas?" "Yes it is", he stated. My thoughts began racing. I immediately became furious thinking what a tragedy that was in that little town, and how I could go ahead and take this guy out myself, or even send the control picket officer on a meaningless errand away from the wing and while I'm in the control picket, "accidentally" open his cell door along with about six other black inmate's doors. I had to do some heavy meditating to calm myself down. And besides, this man was already receiving nationwide media attention, and it was my job to protect all inmates, even from each other.

Time and time again, I was the victim of ill plots, stupid and worthless setups. I was always taught to "turn the other cheek", however I turned the other cheek so often, until that was no longer an option. I was sick and tired of always having to watch my back. All I ever wanted to do was go to work, do my job to the best of my ability, and go home to my family. I did not think that was asking too much.

While assigned to work a gate position, I knew that there were a bunch of officers on eight building with sergeant Fitzgerald. I left my position and went there and said to sergeant Fitzgerald, "hey sarge look, I know that you and sergeant Shields do not really care for me, but I am not worried about that. What I am worried about is that there is an inmate who is housed on B-block that I need to settle a score with". Sergeant Fitzgerald looked directly into my face and I could tell that he was trying not to crack a smile. "Look sarge, I'll go down there, take care of my business and be gone, and nobody will know nothing". Sergeant Fitzgerald stepped aside and stated in a slick tone of voice "take care of your business". I went onto B-block, went right up to the cell, went in, and all that was heard was struggling, what sounded like punches landing, keys, and while taking care of my business, I was even yelling at the inmate asking him, who was the boss! After about twenty seconds, I glanced at the dayroom and saw about six officers present. I then yelled at the inmate saying "oh you got cash money, huh? Where did you get this from?" Immediately about four officers, sergeant Shields, and sergeant Fitzgerald came into the cell where there was about one hundred and thirty dollars cash scattered on the floor. They immediately picked it up. A couple of them got a few sucker punches in on the inmate, and we all exited the cell, breathing hard and laughing. I glanced at sergeant Shields, and he was not laughing at all. I then returned to my gate position, as if nothing had happened, and continued my duties. About thirty minutes later, lieutenant Walker from the internal affairs department, and the assistant warden came up to me and asked me to come with them. I was nervous and scared. Once inside the assistant wardens office, lieutenant Walker stated to me that sergeant Shields called and reported to him that I was involved in a use of force and that I did not report it, in an attempt to cover it up. He then explained to me that sergeant Shields stated he had witnesses, and the only thing that could happened to me is I could be fired, and arrested, because failing to report a major use of force on an inmate is grounds for dismissal, and possible charges filed. By now my face was covered in sweat, and I asked the assistant warden if he could call the head warden in to talk to me before they transported me to the local city jail. The head warden came into the office and looked at me and said, "Officer Hampton, was it worth it?" After a long pause, I stated while smiling and showing nearly all my teeth, "yes sir, it was!" The warden then asked the lieutenant if he had a transport car ready. "Yes sir, I do". Lieutenant Walker stated, "well you better make it a van, because you are going to be taking several of them!" The warden then explained how I went to him about the problems I was having on the unit and how I was a target. The warden also explained that I had planned the whole incident and that I was not guilty of anything. When the four officers and two sergeants came into the office they were read their rights, and they immediately started denying everything. The warden instructed them to empty their pockets, and out came money from each of them. They all claimed that the money was rightfully theirs and the warden reached into his pocket and pulled out a piece of paper and stated, "funny thing I have the serial numbers to all those bills written on this paper." I then stated, " yeah he gave those to that inmate the evening before. Sergeant Fitzgerald then stated, " Hampton beat up the inmate." I then said, "I never touched that inmate, what you all heard was me clapping my hands and yelling. You guys hit that inmate, who volunteered for this operation, and you guys are the ones who had the unreported use of force". Sergeant Shields then said, " we didn't even touch that inmate," I stated, "sure you guys did, and just before shift change this morning, Mr. Petry went inside of the cell across the catwalk and set cameras up to film the whole incident!" The group was taken away in handcuffs, never to return.

One day while thinking about all the things that were planned against me, I felt that it was time to strike back. I had to come up with a plan to get rid of "them", and I only had one chance. I had to get the entire group as a whole.

# XI

# CROOKED OFFICER

In the training academy, several of our instructors told us about the conspiracies that some officers participate in. Sometimes they get away with them, but most of the time they are caught. Our instructors informed us that it is illegal and unjustifiable to get involved in such acts as bringing tobacco or any drugs into the prison unit, or engaging in sexual activities. However, there were still a small percentage of officers who did not take heed to the consequences of getting caught. I remember there was one time when I was working with a male officer who showed me five one hundred dollar bills. I asked him why did he bring in so much cash, and he grinned at me and stated while moving closer to me in a lower tone of voice, "I got this money from in here." I was surprised at what I had just heard. He explained to me that there was plenty of money floating around this penitentiary and that I should get my piece of the pie. I asked this sly and daring officer just how did he manage to conquer such task, and he said, "Man I get twenty bucks for one pack of cigarettes and one hundred bucks for a sack of weed." At the time I was hearing these things, all I could think about was how stupid could this piece of a correctional officer be? I am thinking, he will get three and four hundred dollars here and there, but when he gets caught, he will miss out on two thousand dollars a month, which he was earning honestly. Furthermore, he just might end up in the penitentiary as a result of his wrong doings. I then just stood there wondering as he walked away, what if I report him to my supervisor? I will be called a snitch, and if I do not report him, it's possible me or another officer could get into a confrontation with an inmate who is under the influence of drugs.

Another incident that occurred once before was when I was assigned to work with a female officer. At the beginning of the day, I noticed that she stood at cell number six for about two hours conversing with the inmate who was assigned there. The only time she left from the front of that cell was when she had to count the other inmates or change the television channel. About two hours before quitting time, the female officer came to the control picked to talk to me. I knew that she was just there to see how suspicious I was of her. I played it off and told her that I was asleep inside the air-conditioned picket and paid little attention to her. She fell for my story and she said, "Well I have been talking to the inmate inside of six cell and I stood there a while because I think I smelled tobacco smoke. I am going inside to search the cell from top to bottom, so if you do not see me for a while, do not panic." I then watched her as she again went up to six cell and opened the door. She went inside but I never saw the inmate leave out as they are supposed to do when we are searching their cell. Ten minutes before the next shift comes on to relieve us, the two officers on the cell block usually go over their paperwork making sure what we write coincides with the activities for that day. Well, it was five minutes before quitting time and I pushed the panic button. I called for her over the intercom and I heard what sounded like a belt buckle rattling. I then saw the female officer come out of the cell and close it behind her. She came to the picket and never looked me in the face as she just handed me her paperwork. I felt embarrassed and hurt for my beautiful African American princess who obviously has fallen in love with an inmate who could not do anything for her at the present time, and still allowed herself to be in a situation where she could be accused of having sex with him. I left work that day and still to this day I ask myself, "What do I do, what can I say?"

As days passed, I often thought about this incident. I was taught in training academy that if we are involved in a sexual activity with an inmate, or know of another officer who is, we are to immediately report it. This female officer was a single mother of two young children. I was the father of a three-year old baby girl. If I report what I saw, she would be fired. If I didn't and others found out, I could be fired. This bothered me deeply. One day while eating in the O.D.R., several officers came in talking and laughing. I asked them what was going on, and they told me that the very same female officer who bothered my conscience was fired because an inmate that she had a sexual relationship with gave a letter she had previously written him to a high ranking official in exchange for a minor disciplinary action being removed from his conduct record.

# XII

# OTHER SIDE OF THE WALL

What about life on the outside of prison? Well now that I am in my fifth year being a correctional officer, I can't help but notice the way I talk, think, and act is just like a convict. I sometimes talk in penitentiary language. When I am around my coworkers, most of the things I say they will understand. For example, if I ask one of them to "Shoot me something" such as a soda, money or whatever I name, they will give it to me because "shoot" in penitentiary talk means "give" or "send". I remember once my grandfather asked me for a couple of bucks and I said to him "After I come from the store I will shoot you the change." He became frightened and said to just forget it. He had no idea that I meant well, however, I did not get a chance to explain. There are also other terms such as "That's a bad joker" which means whatever thing your talking is actually good. And if you told me that number twenty-three was one of the greatest basketball players of all time, instead of me saying, "You are right." I would probably say "All the time" which in penitentiary talk means the same thing.

Then there are times when I am shopping and I try to make deals with the salesperson, knowing they do not bargain. The way a convict thinks is on a level higher than the average person. His entire goal is to get over on anyone he can. So in the end he comes out on top. I found myself thinking a lot like this. Do not even talk about the way I act sometimes, because most of the time I am just being silly. Like when my friends ask me for money and I give them blank envelopes and cigarettes. Or when we see an attractive female, we put our hands in our pockets. They are just in our pockets, but when an inmate has his hands in his pockets because he has just seen or see a female, they are not motionless. Damn, I do not know if this penitentiary has made or broken me, but sometimes it can get interesting or disturbing. Then there is the fact that there are guys and girls who are roaming free in society who had done time in prison. The hard part about it is recognizing them because they are no longer dressed in all white, and a few of them have revenge on their mind for officers who treated them bad, like myself in the first couple of years I was employed.

Fly shoes, starched blue jeans, fresh shirt, gold chain, fresh haircut, driving my ninety seven that I just put chrome rims on the week before and one of the prettiest "yellow-boned" girls in all of southeast Texas on the passenger side. I am on my way to go and see a movie with my girl, when I stopped to a store for some gas. I went inside to pay for my gas as my girl sat in the car looking into the visor mirror, putting the finishing touches on her lipstick. When I came out and started fueling my tank, a black old school G-ride drove up, stereo system booming so hard my girl had to stop putting on her lipstick because the mirrors were vibrating. Out of the G-ride stood two middle-aged black dudes. One went inside the store the other looked at me as if he knew me. "Say cuz, ain't your name Hampton?" He asked. I knew that he was an ex-con instantly because everyone in my town knows my first name and everyone in prison knows my last name. "Yeah" I replied as his counterpart came out of the store. He looked at him and said, "This ho ass nigga is a no good motherfucker in prison, but I want to see how crazy he can be out here now." The first thing came to my mind was that they were going to jump me, but whatever they were going to try, I was ready. Then his homeboy grabbed him and I heard him whisper, "Man chill, out - you know we both on parole we cant' be tripping like this

lets just get up out of here, Fuck that nigga."
The other guy had put him in the car and as he
got in on the other side, he stated, "You're lucky"
and they drove off. When I got into my car my
girl was scared and asked what that was about. I
explained to her that was obviously an ex-
inmate from my job who had gotten out of
prison before I decided to change my life
around. He did not get to see the real Officer
Hampton and all he remembered was the dirty
Officer Hampton who I had put behind me.

This made me realize that outside the prison
there are no disciplinary reports, no video
cameras, and no officers ready to come and
assist you. In the free-world, officers are easily
accessible. In prison, officers are bulletproof,
made of steel. But what we need to realize is
that most inmates will not be in prison forever,
and there are no laws or no protection from ex-
cons on the outside.

# THE LETTER HOME

Dear mama,

I am writing you this letter from the state prison, but do not worry I am not incarcerated, however, there are many times that I feel like I am because of most of the things that I go through. As I sit here, I reminisce how things used to be for us. How you raised me. I know that you often wondered what I would become. I cannot help but wonder if you figured your skinniest son would become a prison guard. Mama, I was so confused when I first took this job because I thought I was a correctional officer, but they made me become a prison guard. I thought it was my duty to be an oppressor and mistreat prisoners until I resorted back to the morals and guidelines that you instilled in me. Then there were the times when I felt like there were people out to get me to make sure I did not succeed at being a positive person. I then remembered how you taught me to have a strong will and determination and let no one stand in the way of what I believed in. Even though they stopped me from becoming a supervisor, I know I will get another chance at it. And the way they show favoritism towards the persons in the "cliques". I am not worried because everybody is going to need somebody sometimes and one day that someone just might be me.

I can truly say that I am ashamed of the way I acted at the beginning and the things I did, but most of the time what was really on my mind was keeping my job. What I will do to make up for that is teach every new officer that comes through here the right way to be a correctional officer and maybe the new good will overpower the old bad.

However, mama, the problem will not stop there. I need to figure out a way to prevent people from coming to this place, it's a dead end here with no hope in the future. I will do the best I can with what little I have but until then all I can do is continue holding my own.

Timothy Hampton was born to Bernell and Russell Jean Hampton in August of 1973. Tim, as he likes to be called, spent 29 years of his life in Port Arthur, Texas where he graduated from Abraham Lincoln High School. Tim also attended Lamar University and majored in Psychology and Criminal Justice. Tim spent a total of ten years working for the State Of Texas prison system, eight years as an officer and two years as a sergeant. He also worked part time as a counselor in a mental health facility. Today Tim is a single proud father of two, a daughter Danielle who resides in Atlanta Georgia, and a son, Canden, who resides in Port Arthur Texas. Tim currently resides in sunny Tampa, Florida where he is a children's crisis counselor. Holding My Own is one of three books Tim wishes to write hoping that it reshapes our way of thinking about certain issues.

I would like to thank Jesus Christ for giving me the tools I need, not only in life, but to write this book. I would like to thank those who encouraged me and believed in me while writing this book. Rebecca for guiding me and starting the typing process, Rekisha for always being there for me when I needed someone to talk to, Tina for creating the website www.holdingmyown.com. All my friends back in Port Arthur, Scooby, Darly, Pastor Gene Winston, Ronnie, Willie ( I'm still the king of Madden) Damon, Daniel, Roland, Bo Gip in Dallas, Gee Money, Jessie, Omar and Ladonna. Thanks to my friends here in Tampa Sisco, Brian, Jack, Moses I love ya'll, thanks for welcoming me to my new home. My family, Sheun, Nolan, Mark, Duchess, Karen, and The Hamptons -- I love you all, My Dad Mr. Bernell Hampton, I love you. Keisha and Page I love you both always simply because you are great mothers! Canden and Danielle I love you both always with all my heart, and daddys going to make you two proud! I love you Uncle Byron and Aunt Denise. To my Mother, Grandparents Russell and Eula Mae DeJohn and my dear cousin John-John rest in peace -- I miss you all.

For a copy of Holding My Own send a check or money order for $10.95 to:

I Opening Productions
P.O. Box 270009
Tampa, Florida 33688-0009

Sales tax, shipping and handling included in price of book.